The Rockwool Foundation Research Unit

The wage effect of a social experiment on intensified active labor market policies

Signe Hald Andersen

University Press of Southern Denmark
Odense 2013

The wage effect of a social experiment on intensified
active labor market policies

Study Paper No. 49

Published by:
© The Rockwool Foundation Research Unit and
University Press of Southern Denmark

Copying from this book is permitted only within
institutions that have agreements with CopyDan,
and only in accordance with the limitations laid
down in the agreement

Address:
The Rockwool Foundation Research Unit
Sølvgade 10, 2nd floor
DK-1307 Copenhagen K

Telephone   +45 33 34 48 00

Fax   +45 33 34 48 99

E-mail   forskningsenheden@rff.dk

Home page   www.rff.dk

ISBN 978-87-90199-80-7
ISSN 0908-3979
April 2013
Print run: 300
Printed by: Specialtrykkeriet Viborg

Price: 60,00 DKK, including 25% VAT

Contents

Introduction 6

Background 8
    The experiment. 9

Data 10
    Method. 11
    Outcome. 11
    Treatment status. 14
    Exclusion restriction 14
    Control variables. 15

Results 16

Conclusion 19

References 21

The wage effect of a social experiment on intensified active labor market policies

Signe Hald Andersen (sha@rff.dk)
Rockwool Foundation Research Unit

Abstract

This paper investigates the effect of intensified ALMPs, by increasing the threat of program participation, on post-unemployment wages. For this purpose, we exploit a social experiment conducted in two Danish counties, where approximately 5,000 unemployed people were randomly selected to receive either a standard treatment or an intensified treatment. We use a Heckman selection model and find that an intensified threat of program participation increases the probability of finding a job in the short run, but decreases wages in the same period.

Introduction

We now know that part of the effects of active labor market programs (the so-called ALMPs) aimed at unemployed people can be ascribed to the threat of program participation, rather than to the effect of actual participation (for a review, see Andersen, 2013). In fact, the consequences of this threat may constitute the biggest or even the only effect of such programs. Eberwein et al. (1997), for instance, show that American women, who receive some form of public assistance and who are randomly assigned to participate in a program, have shorter unemployment spells than other similar women receiving public assistance, regardless whether or not they participate in a program. Moreover, Richardson (2002) uses a regression discontinuity model to show that unemployed young Australians are more likely to leave unemployment when they face mandatory training. Lalive et al. (2000) uses a timing-of-event model to show an increase in the probability that Swiss unemployed people exit unemployment when they learn about their obligation to participate in ALMPs (see also Carling et al., 1996). More recently, Rosholm and Svarer (2008), Geerdsen and Holm (2007), Geerdsen (2006), Graversen and van Ours (2008), and Rosholm (2008) have found substantive evidence of a threat effect.

Most studies on threat effects of ALMPs use exit from unemployment as their outcome variable. An exception to this is Black et al. (2003), who analyze how the threat effect influences post-unemployment wages. This is an important focus, as it helps us understand more exactly how the treat effect works. On the one hand, the threat effect may incline the unemployed to lower their reservation wages and accept jobs below their previous wage level. The financial contribution to society of these individuals is then lower than their potential. On the other hand, the threat effect may increase the job search intensity of the unemployed and cause them to find jobs at their initial reservation wage level, but at an earlier time. In this case, the threat effect is the result of increased motivation that prevents potential human capital loss experienced during prolonged unemployment. Here, Black et al. (2003) show that unemployed, who are randomly assigned to participate in a program, have higher post-unemployment wages than similar unemployed, who do not face program participation. However, the difference levels out over time. Also a small group of other studies analyse the question. Here Hägglund (2009) finds that that unemployed, who are randomly assigned to more intense – and thus more threatening – ALMPs, obtain higher wages than unemployed, who receive the standard package. Both studies then support the latter explanation. In contrast, a recent study by Graversen & van Ours (2011) finds no evidence of a threat effect on wages: Using a social experiment conducted in two Danish counties in 2005 and 2006, they find no evidence that a treatment group of newly unemployed, who were randomly allocated to intensive ALMPs, experienced higher or lower wages than a control group of newly unemployed, who received standard ALMPs (see also Klepinger et al., 2002). Cockx & Dejemeppe (2010) test the effect of increased monitoring of unemployed in Belgium. With a reform in 2004, people who had been unemployed for more than a year were informed of a meeting with their caseworker planned to take place in the 21st month of unemployment. This mild threat of monitoring increased exits from unemployment to low wage jobs in some geographical areas and to low as well as high wage jobs in other geographical areas. In similar vein, Johnson & Klepinger (1994) show that unemployed who experience less strict monitoring have the highest wages in their post-unemployment jobs. This suggests that the lesser the threat the better the post-unemployment wage level. In total, the findings of these previous studies support both explanations mentioned above.[1]

However, wage effects are not the main focus of any of these papers, which means that they refrain from investigating the various elements of the findings. One important element is whether differences in wages result from differences in the share of treated unemployed that work, or from the wage they receive. This distinction is quite important, as it will help us understand exactly how the threat effect works. This paper extends the limited literature on the causal effect of the threat of program participation on subsequent wages. Thus, rather than looking at mean differences in wages between treated and

---

[1] Note that the related literature on the effect of benefit exhaustion has focused on earnings effects. Here Arni et al. (2009), for instance, show that the prospect of benefit exhaustion causes unemployed to accept jobs with lower earnings, and van den Berg & Wikström (2009) show that Swedish unemployed are likely to exit to lower wage jobs when they experience sanctions that lower their benefit.

controls, as the previous studies have done, this paper applies a Heckman selection model, that separates the job effect from the wage effect. I exploit the same experiment as the one used in Graversen & van Ours (2008) and Rosholm (2008) which is useful, as previous studies show that the treatment of this experiment had a strong threat effect (e.g. Graversen & van Ours, 2008; Rosholm, 2008).

Background

Theoretically, we can think of a number of ways in which the threat effect of intensified ALMPs could affect the wages of the treated: First, from previous studies we know that an increased threat of ALMPs inclines the unemployed to leave unemployment faster than otherwise. However, this exit from unemployment could either lead to an entry into employment (as suggested by Black et al., 2003) or an entry into other types of public benefit schemes, e.g. sick leave benefits or dropping out of the labor force with no benefits (see Henningsen, 2008). In the first case, the threat effect is likely to increase post-unemployment wages (as there will in fact be wages), whereas in the latter case, wages are unaffected (as there are no wages).

Second, if the exit from unemployment equals an entry into employment, we may observe two wage effects. On the one hand, the threat makes the unemployed anxious to find reemployment, which could cause them to lower their reservation wages. Here, Rosholm & Svarer (2008) suggest that the threat effect might incline unemployed to become less picky with respect to the quality of the jobs, just as van den Berg et al. (2008) show that the prospect of mandatory program participation encourages the unemployed to lower their reservation wages (van den Berg et al., 2008). In that case, intensified ALMPs decrease wages for the treated compared to the controls. On the other hand, the threat may intensify the job search efforts of unemployed people and thereby make them more likely to find work. This shortens the duration of the unemployment, prevents potential deterioration of human capital, and causes less scarring of the unemployed person's wage potential. In this situation the intensified ALMPs increase wages for the treated compared to the controls in the short run (as the controls stay unemployed during months where the treated are already working).

Obviously, all phases and effects exist and may be realized; while some exits from unemployment may lead to entries into employment, other exits may lead to entries into to other public benefit schemes, and this will then be an indication of a heterogeneous effect. Lalive and Zehnder (2007) suggest that the two wage scenarios coexist and net out each other. In the data, it will appear as if there is no threat effect on wages. Yet, another possibility is that one effect dominates in the short run while the other dominates in the long run. The ambition of this study is to assess whether there is one dominant threat effect of ALMPs on post-unemployment wages when looking both at short and long term effects. Given this ambition, we cannot simply compare mean wages of treated and controls, as done in e.g. Graversen & van Ours (2011), rather we need to separate the job effect from the wage effect.

The experiment

To investigate these mechanisms we use Danish administrative data from a controlled social experiment, which the Public Employment Service (PES) conducted in two Danish counties (Sønderjylland and Storstrøm) from November 2005 to March 2006. In this experiment, all persons who became newly unemployed[2] UI recipients[3] during the four months of the experiment were randomly selected to participate in either standard ALMPs or intensified ALMPs. The day of birth determined the random selection, as newly unemployed born in the first half of a month (from the 1st to the 15th of a month) received the treatment, and newly unemployed born in the second half of a month (from the 16th to the 30th/31st of a month) acted as controls (Graversen & van Ours (2008) and Rosholm (2008) describe the experiment).

The aim of the experiment was to investigate whether intensified ALMPs affected the job search behavior of the unemployed. The control group received the standard package of

---

[2] A person is 'newly unemployed' when he or she has not been unemployed in the past 12 months prior to the current unemployment.

[3] These are the insured unemployed, i.e. those who have insured themselves against unemployment prior to the event, wherefore they receive unemployment insurance benefits rather than welfare benefits during their unemployment. Unemployment insurance benefits are higher than welfare benefits.

ALMPs, which included meetings with caseworkers every third month and participation in activation programs after 12 months of unemployment. The law on active labor market policies also allowed the unemployed individuals to participate in a six-week long labor market program of their own choice during the first year of unemployment.

The treatment group faced far stricter measures, which differed from the standard measures in four ways. First, after one and a half weeks of unemployment, the treatment group received a letter informing them that they were part of an experiment and the activities involved in the programs were explained. Second, after five or six weeks, the treatment group members were obliged to participate in a job search program of two weeks duration, and after this program the treatment group had to attend meetings with their caseworker every week or every second week. Third, the people in the treatment group had to participate in a training program of at least three months duration, before the end of the fourth month of unemployment. Fourth, if the people in the treatment group had not found work within six to seven months, their meetings with the caseworker were intensified still further with the purpose of re-evaluating their job search strategy and introducing new active measures (i.e. new activation programs).

Previous studies by Graversen & van Ours (2008) and Rosholm (2008) show that this specific experiment has a considerable threat effect on the unemployed: The treated unemployed exit unemployment considerably earlier than the controls. In addition, Rosholm (2008) finds conclusive evidence that the increased risk of program participation, i.e. the threat effect, explains this observation, as the unemployed tend to leave unemployment just prior to program participation. The experiment is therefore useful for assessing the consequences of the threat effect on post-unemployment wages.

Data

In the analysis we use data from administrative sources: In Denmark all residents have a unique personal number that identifies the resident in a great many transactions, such as interactions with the welfare system, place of residence, work status and criminal behavior. Statistics Denmark conducts a yearly collection of the information registered by this personal number and makes these data available for statistical and research purposes. The available data go as far back as 1980 and comprise all Danish residents. In addition, we have exact information from the PES on the experiment participants. All in all, 5,180 unemployed people were involved in the experiment, either as controls or as treated. As in Graversen & van Ours (2008) and Rosholm (2008), we exclude those who do not stay unemployed for long enough to receive unemployment benefits. This leaves us with 4,712 observations.

Method

As discussed earlier, the process through which increased threats of ALMPs may affect post-unemployment wages consists of two steps: At the first step increased threats affect the probability of exiting to employment, and at the second step, the threats affect the wage offers the unemployed receives and accepts. To investigate this process we therefore apply a Heckman selection model: With this model we may assess, first, if facing the threat of intensified ALMPs affects whether the unemployed person finds employment (i.e. has wages), and second, what the program effect on wages is for those who have wages above 0 (see Heckman, 1979).

Outcome

We assess the wage effect of the experiment using monthly wages, and, given the scope of the Heckman selection model, we utilize two dimensions of this measure: 1) whether or not there is a wage in a given month (i.e. the employment effect), and 2) the specific amount of DKK earned that month (i.e. the wage effect). From the data we know the monthly wage from the start of the experiment until December 2007. The 21st month after the beginning of the unemployment is thus the last month of wages which we can observe for all unemployed in the data. For those entering the program in the last week of the experiment (i.e. first week of March 2006), the 21st month after the beginning of the unemployment spell is also the last month with wage information in our data. Note that due to the registrational practice of Statistics Denmark we only have wages for unemployed exiting to private sector jobs. However, we assume that treated and controls are equally likely to exit to public sector jobs (in the absence of the experiment).

Figures 1 and 2 show differences in monthly wages between the controls and the treated. Figure 1 shows the share of the treated and the controls, which has wages (is employed) by month from the start of the unemployment, and Figure 2 shows differences in average wages, also by month from start of the unemployment. The figures reveal an interesting pattern; from Figure 1 we learn that while the share of employed individuals follows the same pattern in both groups, more individuals in the treatment group are employed – or have wages – each month. Though the difference seems to narrow and almost disappear over time, it is statistically significant until month 19.

Figure 1: Differences in share of employed

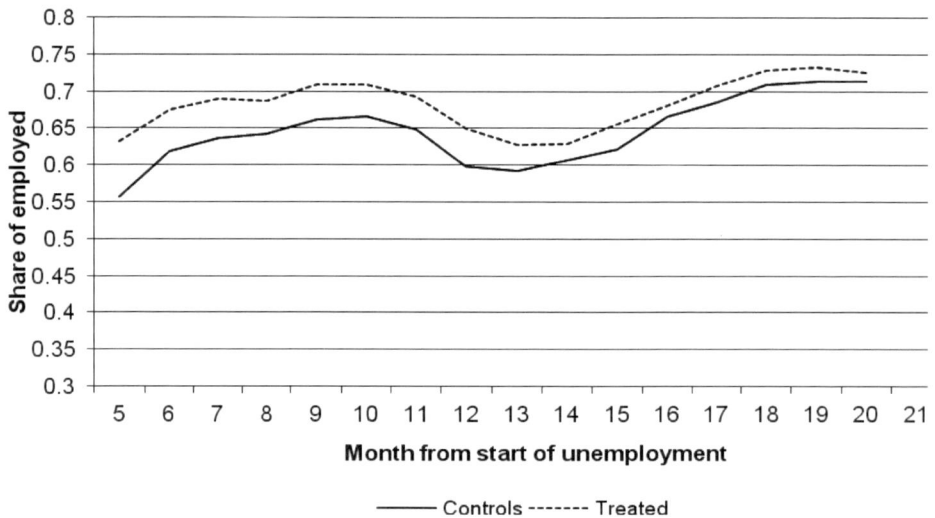

Note: Own calculations based on data from statistics Denmark and the Public Employment Service

As shown in Figure 2, the wage pattern is also the same in the two groups, but individuals in the treatment group have higher wages until month 18. However, the difference is only statistically significant until month 12.

Figure 2: Differences in average monthly wages

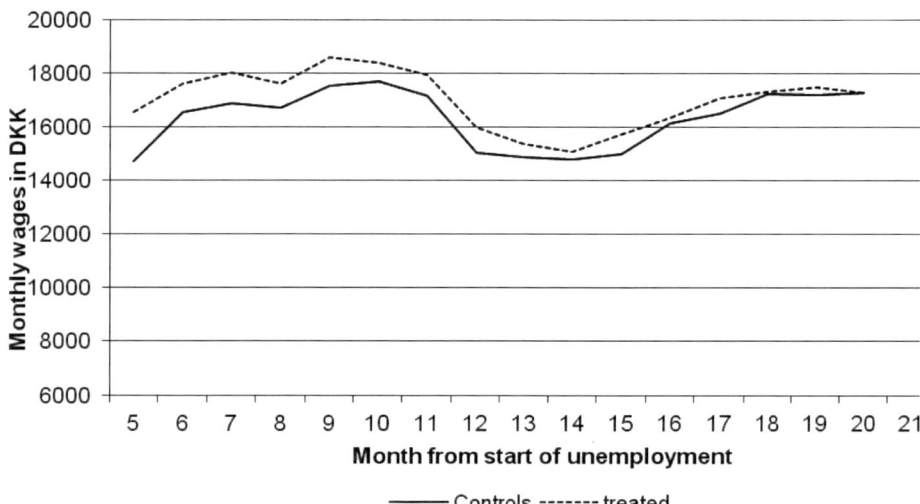

Note: Own calculations based on data from statistics Denmark and the Public Employment Service

Thus, both the wage effect of receiving intensified ALMPs as well as the employment effect wears off over time, at least at this descriptive level. This suggests that experiencing an increased threat of ALMPs reduces the scarring effect of unemployment only in the short run.

Importantly, there are no indications of differences in wages between the treated and the controls prior to the unemployment (as expected given the design of the experiment), as indicated in Table 1.

For the regression analysis, we focus on six months and use wages for 5, 6, 12, 13, 18, and 19 months after the beginning of the unemployment spell as outcome variables in six separate models. We focus on these six points in time to show short (5 and 6 months), intermediate (12 and 13 months) and long (18 and 19 months) term effects of the experiment. We use two measures for each time period to demonstrate that any asserted short, intermediate, and long term effect does not hinge on the specific choice of month. We use logged wages, as is customary in wage regressions.

Treatment status

We indicate treatment status with a binary variable that takes the value 1 for unemployed who were randomly assigned to receive intensified ALMPs and the value 0 for unemployed who were randomly assigned to receive standard ALMPs. As shown in Table 1, in our sample, 2,328 individuals (50.5 percent) received the treatment, while 2,384 individuals (49.5 percent) acted as controls.

Exclusion restriction

To facilitate proper identification, the Heckman selection model requires an exclusion restriction. However, a basic assumption in search models is that anything that affects search intensity (i.e. whether the person finds a job) also affects reservation wage. Thus by definition, we can never find an exclusion restriction for use in the selection model that does not affect the wage equation. The solution is to include an exclusion restriction in the wage equation, and thus find something which we believe affects wages, but not search intensity (Kiefer & Neumann, 1979)

In our analysis we use previous wages as our exclusion restriction. It is our assumption that previous wages do not affect the intensity by which a person looks for a job. Wages received prior to unemployment set the living standard of each individual, and there is no reason to believe that e.g. those with high previous wages are in more need of a job than those with low wages: Both groups need a job which enables them to resume their previous living standard. Furthermore while a high income allows for individual savings – which may provide a safeguard against the financial consequences of unemployment and thus affect search behavior - conservative financial behavior with savings and moderate spending is also not uncommon in low income groups.

In contrast, it is highly likely that previous wages affect the reservation wage of the unemployed. The previous wage will set the standard for the future wage, by guiding the unemployed person's expectations of his or her value at the labor market. This means that the unemployed will depart from the level set by his or her previous wage in wage negotiations with future employers. In addition, the unemployed needs a wage at a certain level to resume his or her previous standard of living, as described above. This all in all suggests that an unemployed person's reservation wage will be strongly correlated with previous wages, but not with job search intensity and that previous wages is a useful exclusion restriction.

Control variables

We show our control variables in Table 1. We include two groups of control variables: The first comprises standard background characteristics like gender, marital status, ethnicity, etc. The second comprises variables related to previous labor market experience of the unemployed, which we assume will also affect future wages, i.e. wages after the unemployment spell under study.

As demonstrated there is only one significant difference between the two groups (there are slightly more immigrants in the treatment group), which indicate that the randomization of the experiment has been widely successful.

Table 1: Variables, descriptive statistics and differences between treated and controls

	Control	Treatment	T-test for differences in means
No. of observations	2,384	2,328	
Gender (1=female)	0.422	0.419	0.166
Married	0.459	0.467	-0.550
Level of education (1-7)	3.358 (1.323)	3.372 (1.305)	-0.356
Children	0.687 (0.997)	0.702 (0.977)	-0.528
Immigrant	0.055	0.069	-1.965*
Exclusion restriction			
Log (wages) prior to unemployment	2.058 (3.318)	1.964 (3.425)	0.963
Controls related to previous labor market experience			
Unemployment in 2004 (0-1.000)	123.377 (184.275)	131.843 (193.133)	-1.540
Tenure, measured in 2004 (0-25.000)	11,413.63 (7,167.3)	11,310.95 (7,179.4)	0.491

*** $p<0.001$; ** $p<0.01$; * $p<0.05$; † $p<0.10$
Note: Own calculations based on data from statistics Denmark and the Public Employment Service

Results

Table 2 shows the results from the Heckman selection model for each of the six outcome measures. The lower panel presents the factors affecting the unemployed people's probability of receiving wages (i.e. the selection model) 5, 6, 12, 13, 18, and 19 months after the beginning of the unemployment spell. The upper panel presents factors influencing wages, provided that the person has wages (i.e. the wage equation).

Looking first at the selection models, we see that an unemployed person's treatment status has a significant effect on the probability that he or she has wages in month 5 and 6 from the beginning of the unemployment spell. Those who receive the treatment are more likely to have wages in the short range.

The results from the selection model show furthermore that women are less likely than men to have wages. Effects of being married and of education are not significant in all models; however, there are indications that married individuals are less likely to have wages and that this probability increases with level of education. In addition, the longer the pre-unemployment tenure and the lower the unemployment in 2004, the more likely the unemployed is to have wages in the months following the beginning of the unemployment spell.

Table 2: The Heckman selection model

Variable	Month 5	Month 6	Month 12	Month 13	Month 18	Month 19
Wage equation						
Treated	-0.085 (0.034)*	-0.077 (0.032)*	-0.085 (0.043)*	-0.057 (0.042)	-0.055 (0.035)	-0.052 (0.035)
Unemployment in 2004 (0-1)	0.107 (0.017)***	0.075 (0.016)***	0.113 (0.021)***	0.106 (0.020)***	0.032 (0.017) †	0.247 (0.017)**
Tenure	-0.047 (0.074)	0.008 (0.071)	0.188 (0.094)*	0.157 (0.092) †	0.071 (0.077)	0.070 (0.078)
Gender (1=female)	0.131 (0.039)***	0.131 (0.037)***	0.046 (0.048)	0.035 (0.047)	0.008 (0.039)	0.014 (0.039)
Married	0.027 (0.037)	-0.002 (0.035)	0.062 (0.047)	0.022 (0.046)	0.005 (0.038)	0.019 (0.038)
Children	0.036 (0.030)	0.049 (0.029) †	-0.009 (0.037)	-0.007 (0.036)	-0.022 (0.030)	-0.034 (0.031)
Immigrant	0.040 (0.086)	0.010 (0.080)	0.270 (0.112)*	0.228 (0.112)*	0.141 (0.086)	0.113 (0.088)
Level of	0.022 (0.006)	0.015 (0.013)	-0.002	-0.011	-0.012	-0.003

education (1-7)			(0.017)	(0.017)	(0.014)	(0.014)
Intercept	10.686	10.493	10.713	10.733	10.445	10.429
	(0.073)***	(0.068)***	(0.090)***	(0.089)***	(0.072)***	(0.073)***
Exclusion restriction						
Log (wages) prior to unemployment	0.022 (0.006)***	0.030 (0.005)***	0.027 (0.007)***	0.027 (0.007)***	0.013 (0.005)*	0.017 (0.005)**
Selection model						
Treated	0.142 (0.052)**	0.122 (0.053)*	0.058 (0.051)	0.052 (0.051)	0.038 (0.052)	0.013 (0.052)
Unemployment in 2004 (0-1)	-0.150 (0.026)***	-0.096 (0.026)***	-0.142 (0.025)***	-0.148 (0.025)***	-0.053 (0.026)*	-0.075 (0.025)**
Tenure	0.311 (0.116)**	0.258 (0.117)*	-0.149 (0.113)	0.022 (0.113)	0.099 (0.116)†	0.046 (0.115)
Gender (1=female)	-0.512 (0.057)***	-0.444 (0.057)***	-0.205 (0.056)***	-0.120 (0.057)*	-0.309 (0.056)***	-0.287 (0.056)***
Married	-0.022 (0.040)	-0.043 (0.057)	-0.082 (0.055)	-0.138 (0.055)*	-0.001 (0.056)†	-0.002 (0.055)
Children	-0.029 (0.056)	-0.033 (0.046)	0.070 (0.045)	0.070 (0.045)	0.066 (0.045)	0.036 (0.045)
Immigrant	-0.177 (0.124)	-0.092 (0.122)	-0.424 (0.125)**	-0.402 (0.127)**	-0.155 (0.121)	-0.254 (0.120)*
Level of education (1-7)	-0.001 (0.021)	0.019 (0.021)	0.041 (0.020)*	0.063 (0.021)***	0.027 (0.020)	0.037 (0.020)†
Intercept	0.123 (0.108)	0.085 (0.108)	-0.224 (0.105)*	0.439 (0.105)***	0.197 (0.106)†	0.163 (0.105)
Athrho	-1.535 (0.056)***	-1.520 (0.054)***	-1.811 (0.053)***	-1.644 (0.052)***	-1.741 (0.048)***	-1.869 (0.054)***
lnsigma	-0.361 (0.025)***	-0.376 (0.023)***	-0.126 (0.024)***	-0.164 (0.026)***	-0.278 (0.021)***	-0.254 (0.020)***
LR test of independent equations (rho=0)	288.49***	295.84***	507.24***	372.15***	518.74***	567.20***
Wald chi^2	68.07***	69.73***	49.67***	47.47***	16.45†	23.29***

*** p<0.001; ** p< 0.01; * p<0.05; † p<0.10
Note: Own calculations based on data from statistics Denmark and the Public Employment Service

Moving on to the wage equation, we see interesting results that go against the immediate intuition of Figure 2. We see significant effects of treatment status on wages in months 5, 6 and 12, but they are negative. That is, though the threat effect of the intensified programs seems to push more people into work, they seem to accept lower paid jobs. This means that on average our group of treated individuals has higher wages than the controls, but only because more have jobs. This finding is further illustrated in Figures 3a-3f, where the grey line marks the average wages at the 5, 10, 15, etc. percentile for the treated, and the dark line marks the average wages at the 5, 10, 15, etc. percentile for the controls. The figures clearly illustrate that more treated have wages, but also that they typically occupy low-wage jobs. However, the figures also illustrate that in the longer run the controls catch up by occupying more and more low wage jobs over time (as the gap between the two lines narrows from figure to figure). This suggests that the threat effect primarily affects unemployed who aspire to low wage jobs (for one or the other reason) and who are otherwise slower in exiting unemployment. This group of unemployed would also experience the lowest gain in income from finding a job.

Based on the figures we cannot determine whether the treated lower their reservation wage as a result of the threat or whether they simply exit unemployment at a faster pace – to a job with the same wage level as they would eventually obtain. If the treated do lower their reservation wage in the short run, they only lower it to a level to which the controls will eventually also lower their reservation. Thus, unemployed receiving increased threats do not seem to suffer from lower wage levels in the longer run and they will earn more in total, as they exit unemployment faster.

Figure 3a: Wages month 5

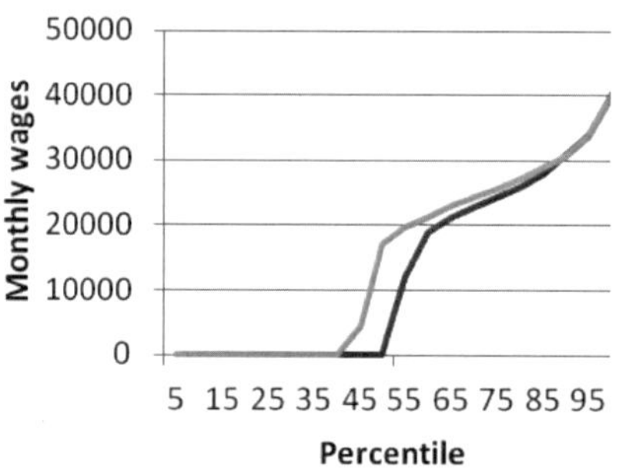

Figure 3b: Wages month 6

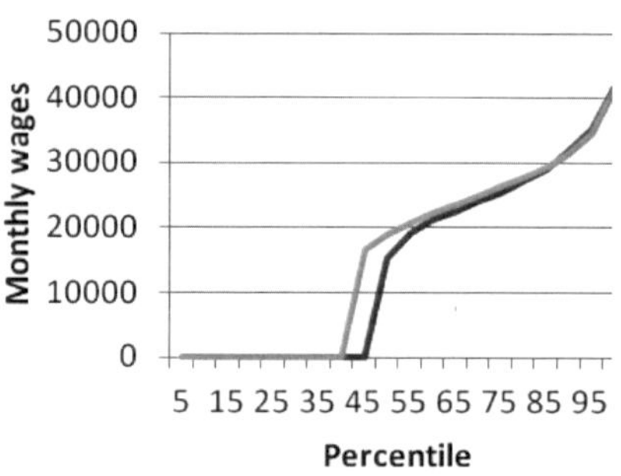

Figure 3c: Wages month 12

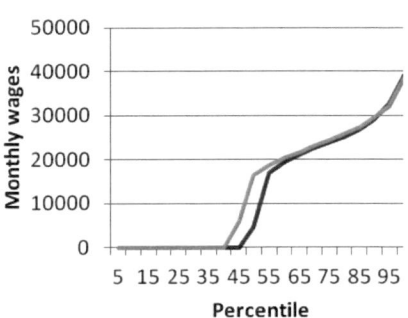

Figure 3d: Wages month 13

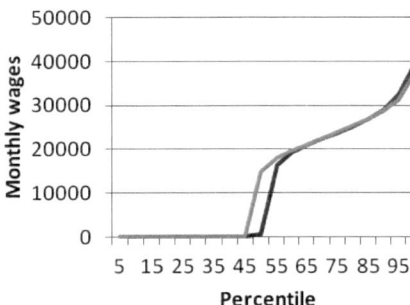

Figure 3e: Wages month 18

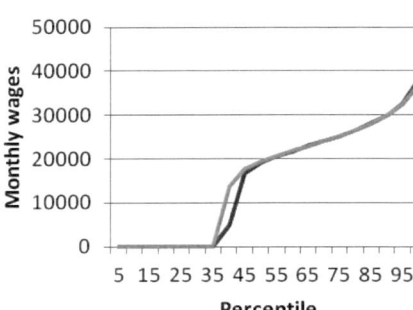

Figure 3f: Wages month 19

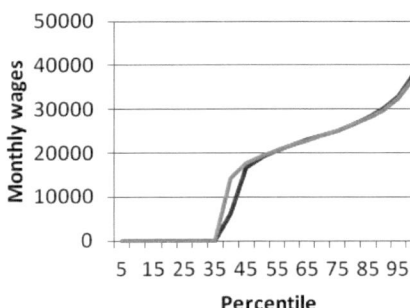

Note: Own calculations based on data from statistics Denmark and the Public Employment Service

The results from the wage equation also show that women earn more than men – at least in the short run. Wages increase by previous labor market experience, but also, and curiously, by previous unemployment. Last, the exclusion restriction is significant in all models, indicating that pre- and post-unemployment wages are positively correlated.

Conclusion

This paper analyses how intensified ALMPs, which strengthen the presence of the threat of program participation for unemployed, affect post-unemployment wages in the short, intermediate, and long run. We show that the threat effect has short run implications both by increasing the probability that the unemployed finds employment (i.e. has wages) and by affecting the actual level of wages. Interestingly, the threat effect lowers wages for those who are quick to find a job. However, it seems to result from more unemployed exiting to low wage jobs fast, which could result from one of two processes; either the threat effect inclines unemployed to accept jobs with lower pay, or it pushes unemployed with lower wages potential into jobs at an earlier stage of their unemployment. When observing that the wage pattern of the control group converges to that of the treatment group over time, the latter explanation seems more appropriate. If this interpretation is valid, the threat effect does not seem to make a difference with regards to the wage levels of the unemployed once they all have a job, but only affects when they exit to employment. Another consequence of this finding is that prolonged unemployment does not seem to have a scare effect.

Importantly, my findings are in opposition to the findings of the previous studies by both Black et al. (2003) and Hägglund (2009), who find positive effects of threat on wages. They are also in opposition to previous studies by Graversen & van Ours (2009) and by Klepinger et al., 2002, who find no effect. However, my findings are in line with the studies by Cockx & Dejemeppe (2010) and Johnson & Klepinger (1994), who find that the threat inclines the unemployed to exit unemployment to lower paid jobs. Like Black et al. (2003), I also find the treatment effect diminishes over time, though with opposite signs. Since mine is the first study to separate job finding from actual wages, the studies are not directly comparable.

References

Andersen, S.H. (2013): How scary is it? – Review of literature on the threat effect of active labor market programs. *Rockwool Foundation Reseach Unit and University Press of Southern Denmark*, Study Paper no. 48.

Arni, P., Lalive, R. & van Ours, J. C. (2009): How Effective Are Unemployment Benefit Sanctions? Looking Beyond Unemployment Exit. *IZA Discussion Paper* 4509.

Black, D. A., Smith, J. A., Berger, M. C. & Noel, B. J. (2003): Is the Threat of Reemployment Services more Effective than the Services Themselves? Evidence from Random Assignment in the UI System. *The Americal Economic Review*, 93(4): 1313-1327

Carling, K, Edin, P.-A., Harkmann, A. & Holmlund, B. (1996): Unemployment duration, unemployment benefits, and labor market programs in Sweden. *Journal of Public Economics*, 59: 313-334.

Cockx, B. & Dejemeppe, M. (2010): The Threat of Monitoring Job Search. A Discontinuity Design. *CESifo Working Paper* no. 3267 (Category 4: Labour Markets)

Eberwein, C., Ham, J. & Lalonde, R. (1997): The Impact of Being Offered and Receiving Classroom Training on the Employment Histories of Disadvantaged Women: Evidence from Experimental Data. *Review of Economic Studies,* 64: 655-682.

Eskelinen, L. & Caswell, D. (2003): *Den socialfaglige praksis ved visitation af arbejdsløse*. Copenhagen: AKF

Geerdsen, L. P. & Holm, A. (2007): Duration of UI periods and the perceived threat effect from labour market programmes. *Labour Economics*, 14(3): 639-652.

Geerdsen, L. P. (2006): Is there a threat effect of labour market programmes? A study of ALMP in the Danish UI system. *Economic Journal*, 116(513): 738-750.

Graversen, B. K. & van Ours, J. C. (2008): How to help unemployed find jobs quickly; Experimental evidence from a mandatory activation program, *Journal of Public Economics*, 92: 2020-2035.

Graversen, B. K. & van Ours, J. C. (2011): An activation program as a stick to job finding, *Labour*, 25: 167-181.

Hägglund, P. (2009): Experimental evidence from intensified placement efforts among unemployed in Sweden. *IFAU Working Paper*, 2009:16.

Henningsen, M. (2008): Benefit shifting: The case of sickness insurance for the unemployed. *Labour Economics*, 12: 1238-1269.

Heckman, J. (1979): Sample selection bias as a specification error. *Econometrica,* 47: 153–61.

Johnson, T. R. & Klepinger, D. (1994): Experimental Evidence on Unemployment Insurance Work-Search Policies. *The Journal of Human Resources*, 29(3): 695-717.

Kiefer, Nicholas M. & Neumann, George R. (1979): *The effect of alternative partial benefits formulas on beneficiary part-time work behavior*. U.S. Dept. of Labor, Employment and Training Administration, Unemployment Insurance Service

Klepinger, D., Johnson, T. R. & Joesch, J. M. (2002): Effects of Unemployment Insurance Work-Search Requirements: The Maryland Experiment. *Industrial and Labor Relations Review*, 56(1): 3-22.

Lalive, R., van Ours, J. C. & Zweimüller, J. (2000): The Impact of Active Labour Market Programs and Benefit Entitlement Rules on the Duration of Unemployment. *IZA Discussion Paper*, No. 149

Lalive, R. & Zehnder, T. (2007): The Effects of Public Employment Programs on Equilibrium Unemployment. Found 13/2-2009 at http://www.eale.nl/Conference2007/programme/Papers%20Friday%2011.00-13.00/add43150.pdf

Richardson, L. L. (2002): Impact of the mutual obligation initiative on the exit behaviour of unemployment benefit recipients: the threat of additional activities. *The Economic Record*, 78(243): 406-421.

Rosholm, M. & Svarer, M. (2008): The threat effect of active labour market programmes. *Scandinavian Journal of Economics*, 110(2): 385-401

van den Berg, G. J., Bergemann, A. & Caliendo, M. (2008): The Effect of Active labor Market Programs on Not-Yet Treated Unemployed Individuals. *IZA Discussion Paper*, No. 3825.

van den Berg, G. J. & Wikström, J. (2009): Monitoring Job Offer Decisions, Punishments, Exit to Work, and Job Quality. *IFAU Working Paper*, 2009:18